CW00544274

SHOUT IT LOUD, SHOUT IT CLEAR

For [illegible]
with best wishes
from John
January 2018.

For my grandchildren
Isabel, Charlie and Coralie
and for my daughters
Marina and Olwen

SHOUT IT LOUD, SHOUT IT CLEAR

Photographs 2014 - 2016

John Comino-James

John Comino-James

DEWI LEWIS PUBLISHING

There may be times when we are powerless to prevent injustice, but there must never be a time when we fail to protest.

ELIE WIESEL

REMEMBER
18TH JAN
1518
DEATHS
IN POLICE
CUSTODY
SINCE 1990
IN ENGLAND AND WALES
0 CONVICTIONS
No more deaths in police custody
Building the independent,

BUS STOP
Whitehall
Trafalgar Square
towards Brixton
3
159
N109
N3
COOL BRITANN
35
COOL
BRITANNIA

The day of the Rugby World Cup Final.

Rugby fans streamed towards inflatable arches to enter the Fanzone in Trafalgar Square. Near the entrance to the underground, relatives and friends of some of those who have died in custody gathered for their silent procession to Downing Street. A woman displayed a tee-shirt declaring statistics in white on black:

1518 DEATHS IN POLICE CUSTODY SINCE 1990
IN ENGLAND AND WALES 0 CONVICTIONS

I made a photograph.

They moved off in silence behind a dozen people holding a two line banner:

UNITED FAMILIES AND FRIENDS CAMPAIGN
NO MORE DEATHS IN CUSTODY

I think of the people I spoke to, and of one man in particular.
He will not remember that I spoke to him.
(He must have spoken to so many).

He will not remember telling me how his brother died.
(He must have told the story so many times).
He will not know that because we spoke I remembered his brother's name.
He will not know that because of the banner he carried I one day recognized his brother's face in the newspaper.
He will not know that because I read about his brother in the newspaper I revisited my photographs, looked up the histories behind the banners.

What is it like to to be told your brother has died in custody?
He will not know (I would like him to know) that because we spoke I followed a trail of names captured in unprinted negatives or discarded photographs and read what I could about those I can never meet:
Joy Gardner, Kingsley Burrell, Ricky Bishop, Sean Rigg, Seni Lewis, Sheku Bayoh, Thomas Orchard, and Jimmy Mubenga.

What is it like to be told your son, your partner, your cousin, your father, your daughter, your mother, your friend, your brother has died in custody?

5 YEAR AFTER Jimmy's DEATH – DEPORTATION BRUTALITY CONTINUES
Jimmy Mubenga RIP
Died 12th Oct 2010 after restraint by private guards hired by the British government on a flight to Angola
STOP FORCED DEPORTATIONS
CLOSE ALL DETENTION CENTRES
JUSTICE + CHANGE NEEDED
BEFORE SOMEONE ELSE DIES
CA'S LAW
TRANSITION
SURVIVAL

Socialist Worker
NO TO RACISM
• Migrants are welcome here
• Stamp out Islamophobia
www.swp.org.uk
STAND UP TO RACISM!
No to Islamophobia
#MuslimLivesMatter
ZONE

Socialist Worker
NO TO RACISM
Stand up to UKIP.org
No to racism
No to bigotry
No to UKIP
RIGHT TO REMAIN
NO HUMAN IS ILLEGAL
righttoremain.org.uk
unite
MIGRATION

DETENTION CENTRES
SHUT THEM DOWN!
RIGHT TO REMAIN
MIGRATION IS BEAUTIFUL
MIGRATION IS A HUMAN RIGHT
MIGRATION IS BEAUTIFUL
ASYLUM

YOU'RE NOT
ANTI-RACIST
IF YOU'RE NOT
ANTI-ZIONIST
International Jewish Anti-Zionist Network
BLACK
LIVES
MATTER
BORDERS
ARE
RACIST!

Stand up
to racism
STAND UP
TO RACISM
Refugees
No to
to war.
Stand up
to racism

WORLD'S BIGGEST RACIST
STAND UP TO RACISM
Refugees welcome here
• No to Islamophobia and anti-Semitism
• Stop scapegoating migrants
Socialist Worker
REFUGEES WELC
• Open the
• Fight racis
Refugees welcome here
Fight against racism and Islamophobia

MIGRATION
IS
BEAUTIFUL
MIGRATION IS A HUMAN RIGHT
No to
Islamophobia.
No to war.
Stop the War Coalition. www.stopwar.org.uk
SocialistWorker
ACKNEY
WE A
hackneym2

THE NATIONAL GALLERY
THE NATIONAL GALLERY
FIGHT RACISM
FIGHT AUSTERITY
ND UP TO RACISM AND FASCISM
RE ALL MIGRANTS
dup2racism@gmail.com

Behind a closed door, the safe twilight of the darkroom. Exposure of sensitive paper under the enlarger's lamp. Under the duress of chemicals detail after detail revealed, intensified. In one image, a row of protesters extends a banner,

CLOSE DOWN YARL'S WOOD AND ALL DETENTION CENTRES

I remember taking the picture: Parliament Square on Magna Carta Day. Photographs developed, fixed, washed, hung up to dry, not an end but a beginning.

And so one afternoon of heat I am in the countryside near Bedford, walking along a rutted track. Cereals ripen around me. Behind a fence behind a fence there it is, Yarl's Wood Immigration Removal Centre. It is described as a fully contained residential centre housing adult women and adult family groups awaiting immigration clearance.

Women held there who have entered the UK seeking asylum, often while fleeing war or sexual violence in their home country.

Women held while their immigration/asylum status is established by the Home Office.

On the track are several hundred demonstrators from all over the country. A decade of complaints about sexual abuse and mistreatment have been documented. Activists demand the closure of detention centres.

We are here because you are there.

A fence of mesh and steel fence surrounds the inner compound. Modern brick buildings, shallow pitched roofs. The upstairs windows appear opaque, they do not open fully.

We cannot see in, but can the women inside see out? Surely by now they can hear the chanting, *"Detention centres, shut them down"*.

Protesters kick the steel panels of the fence. The din drowns out the birds of Bedfordshire.

We are here because you are there.

Suddenly an arm appears, a leg is thrust through the gap where the window is opened to its limit, towels are waved. From one window a toilet roll unravels, trails down like bunting.

Detention no longer a word but a state.
We are here because you are there.

The crowd in a spate of emotion, of anger.

NO HUMAN IS ILLEGAL

NO SISTER IS ILLEGAL
SHUT DOWN

MOVEMENT FOR JUSTICE
WE are here because YOU are there
STOP the scapegoating of immigrants
MOVEMENT FOR JUSTICE
NO to rape
NO to sexual abuse
NO to mental torture
Shut down Yarls Wood

MOVEMENT FOR JUSTICE
NO to rape
NO to sexual abuse
NO to mental torture
MOVEMENT FOR JUSTICE
SHUT
DOWN
YARLSWOO

MOVEMENT FOR JUSTICE
by any means necessary
WE are here
because
YOU are there
STOP the
scapegoating of
immigrants
Notice
Private property
Keep out

Cecil says
ALL PEOPLE
ARE BORN FREE

HUMAN
SHUT
DOWN
YARL'S
WOOD
SHUT
DOWN

TAKE DOWN THIS WALL
FREEDOM NOW
SHUT IT DOWN
صوت
NO ONE IS ILLEGAL

DOWNING STREET SW1
GAZA

FREE PALESTINE
END ISRAELI OCCUPATION
www.palestinecampaign.org
Gaza
Stop the massacre
Stop the War Coalition www.stopwar.org.uk
Palestine Solidarity
FREE PALESTINE
END ISRAELI OCCUPATION
www.palestinecampaign.org
PALESTINE
لفلسطين الحرية
www.socialistworker.co.uk
SocialistWorker
FREEDOM for PALESTINE
لفلسطين
FREE PALESTINE
END ISRAELI OCCUPATION
MURDERER
STOP
ARMING
APARTHEID
ISRAEL

Socialist Worker
FREEDOM
for

GAZA
www.palestinecampaign.org
FREE PALESTINE
END ISRAELI OCCUPATION
www.palestinecampaign.org
ARREST
NETANYAHU
CHILD KILLER
End the siege
Stop the War Coalition www.stopwar.org.uk

My name is
Bisan Abu Jame'
I was killed along with 26 of my cousins, brothers, sisters, aunts and uncles.
I was 6 months old.
#Notinmyname
My name is
Maysaa Abu Jame
I was 7.

ZIONISM
AND
JUDAISM
ARE
DIAMETRICLLY
OPPOSED
www.nkEurope.org
State of "Israel"
DO NOT
Represent
WORLD
JEWRY
www.nkEurope.org
Judaism & Zionism
Are
Diametrically Opposed
JUDAISM = RELIGION.
ZIONISM = NATIONALISM
FREE PALESTINE
FREEDOM PALESTINE
Stop the massacre

Far from the sea, far from the edge of land, a familiar urban landscape of shoppers, tourists, Macdonalds, Boots, Waterstones, cash machines, Clarks, Snappy Snaps. I am swept along in the Saturday crowd. In Gaza shells are exploding, I have seen the battered pick-ups, shattered houses. the ambulances on TV, have been forewarned of images some viewers may find distressing. The ruptured bodies. The blood in the dust of ruined streets. Around me the crowd roars, *"In our thousands in our millions we are all Palestinians"*. I am swept along, but when I try to join in my voice has no authority, *"From the river to the sea, Palestine shall be free"*. Tourists watch us pass, take photographs. There is a child asleep in a pushchair. I cannot find my voice. Someone has made a placard

YOU DON'T NEED TO BE A MUSLIM TO STAND UP FOR GAZA
YOU JUST HAVE TO BE A HUMAN

It dances over the heads of the crowd borne along on the roar of anger, of determination.

I remember an image, a man carrying a broken child. I am a father. I am living a fortunate life. The only dead I have seen have all been complete, unmaimed, presented for my viewing in their undertaker's rouge. My grandchildren are living to outgrow their clothes. I know why I am here.

Afternoon Tea Bus
Gaza
End the siege
Stop the War Coalition www.stopwar.org.uk
Gaza
End the siege
Stop the War Coalition www.stopwar.org.uk
ATTACKS
ON GAZA

GAZA
HEY CAMERON
WHERE WAS YOUR
MILITARY
INTERVENTION
WHEN ISRAEL
PUMMELLED GAZA!

HEID
ng in Palestine
WWW.INMINDS.COM
THE ONGO
EANSING O
MINDS.COM
“We will return.
That is not
a threat
not a wish
a hope
or a dream
but a
promise.
1949-19
22% PALES
GEES DENIED
without
Palestini
NDELA

1215
MAGNA CARTA
2015
GUANTANAMO

SAVE SHAKER AAMER CAMPAIGN
MAGNA CARTA DAY
DEMAND JUSTICE
FOR SHAKER AAMER
FREE SHAKER AAMER
SAVE SHAKER AAMER CAMPAIGN
ssac.contact@btinternet.com 07756493877
SAVE SHAKER AAMER CAMPAIGN
MAGNA CARTA DAY
USA MUST FREE
SHAKER AAMER
BACK TO UK
SAVE SHAKER AAMER CAMPAIGN
ssac.contact@btinternet.com
SAVE SHAKER AAMER CAMPAIGN
MAGNA CARTA DAY
FREE
SHAKER AAMER
SAVE SHAKER AAMER CAMPAIGN
ssac.contact@btinternet.com

UN COMMITTEE FOR TORTURE
TELLS USA
CLOSE
GUANTANAMO
FREE PRISONERS
PROSECUTE THOSE
WHO TORTURE
END THE TORTURE, ABUSE, BEATINGS
SAVE SHAKER AAMER CAMPAIGN
ssac.contact@gmail.com

There are known knowns. These are things we know that we know. There are known unknowns. That is to say, there are things that we know we don't know. But there are also unknown unknowns. There are things we don't know we don't know.

A half-term outing with my granddaughter to Ripley's *Believe it or Not.* Afterwards in Parliament Square we see figures in orange jumpsuits, black hoods. One shouts: *"Free Shaker Aamer now!"* Another shouts: *"Cameron! Obama! Close Guantanamo now!"* I tell my granddaughter there is a man in prison for something he did not do, tell her that that is why the people are there protesting on his behalf.

At Hyde Park corner on a sunny afternoon, a tourist creates a selfie posing with a figure wearing manacles, a black hood, an orange jump-suit. Banners on the railings:

CLOSE GUANTANAMO 10 YEARS OF SHAME

TORTURE A LIFE SENTENCE NO JUDGE OR JURY

They speak to knowns than cannot be un-known: reports from Bagram, Abu Graib, Guantánamo Bay.

An undeniable darkness with no remaining option to believe it or not.

I cannot un-watch *Taxi to the Darkside.*
I cannot un-read *Guantanamo Diary* or *The Guantanamo Files.*
I cannot un-read *Cruel Britannia,* cannot un-feel betrayed by my government's complicity in extraordinary rendition.

There are knowns that cannot be, must never be, unknowns again ....

When Shaker Aamer is flown in to Biggin Hill after 14 years incarceration at Guantánamo Bay, he says *"I feel obliged to every individual who fought for justice not just for me but to bring an end to Guantánamo. Without knowing of their fight I might have given up more than once; I am overwhelmed by what people have done by their actions, their thoughts and their prayers and without their devotion to justice I would not be here in Britain now. The reality may be that we cannot establish peace but we can establish justice. If there is anything that will bring this world to peace, it is to remove injustice."*

Will my granddaughter remember the people in Parliament Square?

FREE TIBET

TAND
UP
R THE
PPRESSED
IN
HINA AND
TIBET
DOWN WITH THE CHINESE COMMUNIST PARTY!
DOWN WITH THE CHINESE COMMUNIST PARTY!
OLICE
CAMERON:
Don't
trade
away
HUMAN RIGHTS
END THE

SILENCE WILL
ONLY SUPPORT
MURDERS

ÇAĞDAŞ AYDIN
MURAT YURTGÜL
POLEN ÜNLÜ
MEDALİ
İSMET ŞEKER
KORAY
H.EZGİ SADET
ALPER SAPAN
SÜLEYMAN AKSU
NURAN KOCA
KASIM DEPREM
OSMAN ÇİÇEK
VEYSEL ÖZDEMİR
BÜŞRA METE
CEMİL YILDIZ
UĞUR ÖZKAN
E. DENİZ EROL
FERDANE KILIÇ
A.EZGİ ŞALCI
NARTHAN KILIÇ
YUNUS EMRE ŞEN
CEBRAİL GÜNEBAKAN

NAZLI
SOLIDARITY WITH KOBANE
JUSTICE FOR SURUÇ...
PROTECT
AGAINST
ISIS

Nkosiyabo Xalabile
At Lonmin since 2004, 30 years old
Shot in thigh and buttock by the police
Mphangeli
Thukuza
MZUKISI SOMPETA
Fezile
Saphendu
At Lonmin since 2009, 24 years old
Shot twice by the police under his arm

INVESTEC - MARIKANA IS
YOUR PROBLEM
DO THE RIGHT THING
• APOLOGISE AND COMPENSATE THE FAMILIES
• PAY THE MINEWORKERS A LIVING WAGE
• IMPLEMENT THE PROMISES ON HOUSING
• STOP AVOIDING CORPORATION TAX IN SOUTH AFRICA
Marikana Miners Solidarity Campaign (UK)

Persecution
Torture Methods
Used on Falun Gong
Practitioners in China
November 20, 2001,
Tiananmen Square,
Beijing, China
3724 People Killed
in China for Their Beliefs
Daddy's gone,
I don't know why.
Fadu's father was tortured to death in China
because of his belief in Falun Gong when she was
15 months old. The sudden tragedy made
her mom's hair turn white overnight.
www.faluninfo.net
www.faluninfo.net
Help Rescue Children
Suffered from Persecution
of Falun Gong in China

STOP
Stop organ
harvesting in
China
www.stoporganharvesting.org
法
好
忍
Forbearance
活摘法輪功
法輪大法

GRIEF &
FOR
ALL SUFFERING
FROM
TUNISIA ATTACK
OXI
SAY NO TO
AUSTERITY &
BLACKMAIL

I stand silent in Whitehall as people take turns to read out from a list the names of over 1400 Palestinians who died as a result of Israeli action in Gaza during the previous summer.

I stand silent outside South Africa House at a ceremony to commemorate the striking miners gunned down at Marikana.

I stop at Piccadilly Circus where demonstrators are sitting in the road. Under the statue of Eros the faces of those who died at Suruc are interspersed with the faces of the living.

All around me are strangers. I wonder what it means to break the easy pace of my life, to let myself turn aside for a few moments, to pay attention at such commemorations, what is it to do with me? What good can it possibly do?

I have heard that Gandhi said: *'Massacre of innocent people is a serious matter. It is not a thing to be easily forgotten. It is our duty to cherish their memory.'*

One Saturday in Trafalgar Square I saw a man holding a placard that read

GRIEF & ♥ FOR ALL SUFFERING FROM TUNISIA ATTACK

I took a photograph.
He looked at no-one in particular.
He was silent.
He was simply there.

DON'T GIVE DOCTORS A LICENCE TO KILL
Beware the Slippery Slope

GIVE ME CHOICE OVER MY DEATH
how many Years a Mortal man may live.

Opposite Old Palace Yard a periwigged marionette raises an admonishing finger: *Beware the Slippery Slope.*

Propped against the railings, a dogmatic assertion:

ASSISTED SUICIDE IS A DENIAL OF GOD'S PROVIDENCE

In a matter of hours Parliament will vote on a Private Members' Bill *'to enable competent adults who are terminally ill to choose to be provided with medically supervised assistance to end their own life…'*

I think of my mother who dreaded the prospect of the pain and indignity and dependency she saw overtake so many of her friends.

I know what her view of the proposal would have been, and I imagine her here with me talking to people who have accompanied their loved ones on their chosen way to Switzerland. I imagine that it is her who is carrying that bag with the legend GIVE ME CHOICE OVER MY DEATH, that it is her walking across the inscription on the Jubilee sundial:

'… how many days will finish up the year, how many years a mortal man may live.'

POLICE

NO. HUMAN
RIGHTS
JUST. CASH
REMBRANDT

Far from the edge of land, far from the sea, a protest against the capture and killing of dolphins. A crowd assembling in Cavendish Square. There are banners, placards:

JAPAN STOP THE DOLPHIN SLAUGHTER

TAIJI LET THEM BE

I meet a couple who have driven all the way up from the West Country, a man making a video: I talk to protestors who have come from Holland. Someone asks if I have watched *The Cove*. The march sets off for the Japanese Embassy in Piccadilly, crosses Oxford Street, and its passionate chant reverberates in Regent Street. *"Shame, shame, shame on Japan."* From behind plate glass, staff in a shop look out as if from a vivarium. Tourists watch us pass, take photographs on mobile phones and iPads. The organizers hope such images will circulate on social media, spreading their message. The chants create an enclosing bubble of sound. *"Stop the slaughter in the water"*. Perhaps even now fishermen from Taiji are banging on steel pipes lowered into the water, confusing a pod of dolphins with a wall of underwater sound. Perhaps even now they are herding the disorientated creatures into the cove, and securing nets to prevent their return to open water. Tomorrow, perhaps, a few females will be selected for sale to trainers, the rest will be slaughtered.

The waters of the cove will run red.
Someone is holding up a placard:

JE SUIS DOLPHIN

BEEP
FOR
DOLHPINS
SAMSUNG
Coca-Cola
TAIJI
COVE
I HATE
TAIJI
COVE GUARDIANS
SEA SHEPHERD
NOT 4 SA

I'M NOT
YOUR
TROPHY
LIONAID
ONEPROTEST
ARE
NOT YOUR
ROAR
for
CECIL !
ROAR

#ANIMALS
ARE
NOTFREIGHT

I am Fox
I am Fox
KEEP THE BAN

bees
Save our bees
38 DEGREES
Honey before money
38 DEGREES
ANNUL THE UNJUST
SANCTIONS ON ERITRE

Dragons
at The Forum
the
forum
STOP

22 JUN – 5 SEP
10am – 6pm | #forumdragons
forum
GoGO DRAGONS!
2015
MARZANO
forum
GoGO
DRAGONS!
2015
GoGoSchools! | 4 Jul – 5 Sep
More than 100 schools and youth groups across Norfolk have decorated their own baby dragons.
They are on show at:
The Forum
intu Chapelfield
Castle Mall
Norwich Lanes shops and other independent retailers.
#forumdragons
Find out which dragon is where online
theforumnorwich.co.uk
Pensthorpe Natural Park
forum
MARZANO
CAFE & BAR
TTIP
itch-up

CHURCHILL
This area is
temporarily closed.
Please keep out.

OCCUPY
DEMOCRACY

Once in a parish election I watched the count, the questioning of doubtful marks, the setting aside of spoiled papers, the declaration of results.

What is it like to live in a country that does not hold free elections, what is it like to live where there is intimidation, where ballot boxes disappear, where the ballot is not secret?

For most of my life I have lived in safe seats: what has my vote, so diligently cast, been worth except in the upholding of a principle?

Others earned me the right to take my turn in the flimsy booth, to pencil my cross against a name, or to spoil the paper: a privilege not to be neglected.

But for all our pride in our commitment to democracy, in May 2015 about a third of the electorate did not vote.

The vast majority of votes cast up and down the land simply do not count. More than half the electorate is unlikely ever to see their constituency change hands.

In May 2015 the votes of about a quarter of the electorate gave the Conservative Party an overall majority in the House of Commons. Power is held by a small minority, and the voting system upholds that status quo.

One day in Old Palace Yard I saw a woman holding a sign she had made:

FOR OVER 40 YEARS MY VOTE HAS BEEN POINTLESS
PR THE WAY FORWARD *

One day in Old Palace Yard I saw a man holding up a placard:

MAKE ELECTIONS FAIRER DAVE!

One day in Old Palace Yard I saw a man holding up a placard:

GREENS & UKIP WON 5 MILLION VOTES BUT ONLY 2 SEATS
NOT DEMOCRATIC

His companion had a sign:

THERE CAN BE NO DEMOCRACY WITHOUT A FAIR VOTING SYSTEM
REFORM THE VOTE

** PR: Proportional Representation*

20 MILLION VOTERS DIDN'T VOTE TORY; THE MANY ARE WATCHING
Socialist Worker
Get the Tories Out!
Strike, protest, occupy
END AUSTERITY

24 HOUR
GENERAL
STRIKE
AGAINST AUSTERITY
END

63% SAID
NO
UNFAIR VOTING
HAS GOT TO
GO
No party should win a majority government with just 37% of the vote.
We want proportional representation where seats match votes and where our parliament reflects who we vote for, not just dictated by a single party.
We are the @63percent
FIRST PAST
THE POST
37% of
the vote
51% of
the MPs
IT'S JUST

DSMITHS
ESTINE
CAMPAIGN
IF THIS
PROTEST WAS
IN EGYPT
YOU'D END UP:
KILLED
INJURED
DETAINED
WHOISSISI.COM
#STOP
SISI

OUR
AUSTERITY
THEIR
PROSPERITY
YE ARE
socialist students
fight for
FREE
EDUCATION
fight for
FREE
EDUCATION

DEFY
TORY
RULE
US ALL
OBS
NOT
TRIDENT
FAREWELL
TO
WELFARE
Dear David
STOP
TELLING
PORKIES
I still hate
Margaret
Thatcher.

CAMERON GETS HIS KICKS FROM THATCHER'S OLD TRICKS
END·AUSTERITY·NOW
OCTOBER 2015 MANCHESTER
Socialist Worker
DEFEND THE RIGHT TO STRIKE
CUT

WORKERS' LIBERTY
workersliberty.org
MAKE CAPITALISM HISTORY
FIGHT FOR SOCIALISM
"Is man one of God's blunders? Or is God one of man's blunders?"
Friedrich Nietzsche
FIGHT AUSTERITY
Unite the Resistance rally after TUC demo
OXI OXI OXI
BALLS TO THIS
NO MORE DEATHS
OXI! NO To Austerity in Greece or ANYWHERE!
Global ♀'s Strike
COPING
IS ALREADY WORK
SAVE INDEPENDENT LIVING FUND!
BENEFIT CUTS SANCTIONS CARE CUTS ARE KILLING US!
WinVisible
REFERENDUM HERE TOO!
CUTS TO BENEFITS WAGES
BENEFIT CAP = MORE DOMESTIC MURDERS

FREE CAKE
AGAINST AUSTERITY
THE PEOPLE'S ASSEMBLY
Stop the privateers
Reinstate Candy
CESS DENIED
NO HOME, JUST CAKE HOME
TO INDEPENDENT
LIVIN
Get the Tories Out!
Strike, protest, occupy
youthfightforjobs.com
Youth Fight AUSTERITY
Strike, protest, occupy
OX

"… it is the mark of a civilized community that it can accommodate protests and demonstrations…"

One September morning in Docklands I photographed as police officers made video recordings of protesters outside the Defence and Security Equipment International Arms Fair.

Today the helicopter I hear ceases its traverse, shifts round on its axis, hovers over the crowd. It hangs like an insect, paying attention to the current of people. It is searching, reaching among the random semaphore of placards. It is feeding an insatiable memory with faces collected in high definition.

I look up and as I track the sound of the rotors I remember the sensation of looking down from a helicopter. I had paid for a few minutes ride at a village fayre. Strapped into the bubble of the cockpit next to the pilot I could look down past my feet as if I had become a disembodied eyeball. A thousand feet below, the houses, the allotments, the roads I used every day, the farms and the fields, spread out in a map I could not immediately orientate.

TUSC AGAINST CUTS
100% ANTI-AUSTERITY
WWW.TUSC.ORG.UK
WHEN THE GOVERNMENT TURNS AGAINST THE PEOPLE, REBELLION IS A RESPONSIBILITY
feed the needy, not the greedy
THORNSETT
CUTS KILL
NO PRIVATISATION AT THE NATIONAL GALLERY
Socialist Worker
Stop the privateers
Reinstate Candy

CUT
THE CRAP
AUSTERITY
KILLS
YOU DON'T KNOW
WHAT YOU GOT
TIL IT'S SOLD
KILL
the
HOUSING
BILL
SECURE HOMES FOR ALL
CONTROL RENTS
BEFORE
PROFIT
BUTTERFIELDS
WON'T
SOCIAL
HOUSING
IS A
NATIONAL
TREASURE

Socialist Worker
DEFEND THE RIGHT TO STRIKE
Kill the Trade Union Bill
www.swp.org.uk
WHAT'S ON

I'm proud to be in a TRADE UNION
Canon

ARTICLE 9:
FREEDOM
OF THOUGHT.
ARTICLE 2:
RIGHT TO LIFE
Socialist Worker
NO TO
RACISM
Liberal
Democrats
Protect
Human Rights
Protect
Human Rights
Liberal
Democrats
SAVE HRA
SAVE FREE
PRESS
Protect
Human Rights
Socialist Worker
NO TO
RACISM
PROTECT
QUEEN MARY

CYNULLIAD Y WERIN CEREDIGION
CEREDIGION PEOPLE'S ASSEMBLY
BANKER'S BONUSES. HOW MUCH? YOU WHAT!?!
END AUSTERITY NOW
TUSC AGAINST CUTS
100% ANTI-AUSTERITY
WWW.TUSC.ORG.UK
TRADE UNIONIST AND SOCIALIST COALITION
Socialist Worker
CUTS KILL END AUSTERITY
Socialist Worker
Get the Tories Out!
I'M A LITTLE UPSET
YOU ARE WRONG
Socialist Worker
CAMERON! WE REVOLT BECAUSE YOU REVOLT US!
AGAINST AUSTERITY
THE PEOPLE'S ASSEMBLY
END AUSTERITY NOW

AGAINST AUSTERITY
THE PEOPLE'S ASSEMBLY
NO CUTS
Socialist Worker
DEFY TORY RULE
HEALTH
CARE
WEALTH
SHARE
REVERSE THE CUTS
US ALL
END AUSTERITY NOW

DEAR TORIES
FUCK OFF
FROM SONJA
WE ARE THE 99%
TAKE THE WEALTH OFF THE 1%
NATIONALISE THE BANKS
Socialist Party
www.socialistparty.org.uk
CCHP NOT FOR SALE
#healthnotwea
FIGHT FOR SOCIALISM
CUTS
US ALL
THATCHERS DEAD PARTY

I'M HERE, I'M QUEER, I CAN'T AFFORD 9K A YEAR!
THEY CUT WE BLEED
EDUCATION NOT MARKETISATION
YOU ARE NOT ALONE
Don't Bomb Syria
CUT WAR NOT WELFARE
FREE EDUCATION
KEEP THE GRANTS
KEEP THE GRANTS
FREE EDUCATION

END AUSTERITY NOW
WHAT WOULD TONY BENN DO?
AUSTERITY KILLS
END AUSTERITY
TORY-BUSTERS
ORGANISE STRIKE RESIST!
LEFT UNITY
NO CUTS
NO BARRIERS
GRANTS NOT DEBT
Rich parents for ALL
THE STUDENT ASSEMBLY AGAINST AUSTERITY
F**K FEES

Where is this BIG SOCIETY?
Traveller RIGHTS Human RIGHTS
#WeSTILLcount

London
Gypsy and
Travellers
STAFFORD CRIPPS ESTATE SAYS
"WE CAN NO LONGER AFFORD
THE TORIES". NO TO TORY
Socialist Worker
Housing for all...
PEOPLE
BEFORE
PROFIT
KILL THE
HELP
PREVENT
HOMLESSNESS
NOT PROMOTE

SAVE
OUR
STEEL
SAVE OUR STEEL
Mirror
CAMPAIGN
Unite
UNION

TATA
Unite
GMB
SAVE OUR STEEL
TATA STEEL

Fight
AUSTERITY
LET'S SHAR
NICEL

SO ANGRY
I MADE
THIS SIGN
A SPOT OF
ANARCHY
WOULD BE
NICE ?
SNP

Gloucestershire
The Future
Don't
FRACK
it up!
Shire Hall (Main Reception
NO
FRACKING
ANYWHERE
FRACK
OFF

WE NEED
SOME
LEADERSHIP
WHAT KIND OF
REATURE SHITS
IS OWN NEST ?

YSTEM
CHANGE

CUT THE
GREED
IN NEE
CUT
FOSSIL FUEL
SUBSIDIES
NOW
IT'S THE
GREEN
ECONOMY
STUPID
NO
YES

SECURITY. STABILIT OPPORTUNITY.
NO
Stop
Heathrow
Expansion
stopheathrowexpansio

RUNWAY
NO IF

And on another day, too far above the land to see, an Airbus A320. Looking out from the cabin I see only the wing and the sky. I can almost count the rivets on the aileron. I do not imagine this crafted metal washing up on a remote beach or being retrieved from a desert landscape strewn with human remains. I read, I eat, I doze. I watch the operation of the flaps, the rearrangement of airflow. Cabin doors to manual and cross check. I give no thought to the wake of noise that the aircraft trails down over the city, the air quality near the airport. I have, after all, bought my ticket at the asking price.

And on another day in Manchester, a sort of carnival aeroplane-dragon is coming towards me down the street. Fabric stretched over hoops, extended wings. Capital letters on the fuselage:

NO 3RD RUNWAY: NO IFS NO BUTS

Protesters have tabards and placards:

STOP HEATHROW EXPANSION

I run ahead as they negotiate bollards and benches, planters of palms and ivy, then turn out of breath, hurrying backwards trying to frame a photograph.

One day someone looking through my pictures tells me how a group of activists broke into a restricted area at Heathrow and chained themselves to fencing on a runway. They have been sent for trial.

Outside the magistrates court I talk to campaigners about the social and environmental consequences if the airport is expanded and a third runway is constructed. Supporters have banners and placards. Passing pedestrians and motorists can get the message:

HEATHROW 13 TOOK ACTION
FOR OUR CLIMATE FOR OUR FUTURE

IF GOVERNMENT WILL NOT PROTECT OUR CLIMATE
ORDINARY RESPONSIBLE PEOPLE HAVE TO TAKE A STAND

At the end of the trial the thirteen, Graham Thompson, Danielle Paffard, Ella Gilbert, Sam Sender, Alistair Tamlit, Rebecca Sanderson, Dr. Rob Basto, Kara Moses, Melanie Strickland, Edward Thacker, Sheila Menon, Cameron Kaye, and Richard Hawkins, are found guilty of aggravated trespass and of entering a security restricted area of an aerodrome without permission. They receive suspended sentences and are ordered to carry out community service. In the words of one of the activists:

"Heathrow and the government keep proving to us that they aren't taking climate change seriously. I want a world without the impacts of catastrophic climate change for my and future generations. If this generation of politicians and decision makers won't take the steps needed to combat CO_2 emissions then it falls to ordinary people like us to take action to protect the planet, ourselves and others around the world"

LISTEN UP NOT LOCK UP
ARE WE REALLY LOCKING UP
OUR PEACEFUL PROTESTERS???
#REDLINE #NONEWRUNWAYS #PLANESTUPID #HEATHROW13

Cavendish

SOLIDARITY
WITH DISABLED
PEOPLE AGAINST
CUTS

MICHAEL WATT
AUGURAL MEETING-1871
THATCHER

NO PRIVATISATION
NHS
SOS
NHS
SOS
LEFT UNITY
BRIGHTON + HOVE
NHS
SOS
Stop cuts, closures and privatisation
www.socialistworker.co.uk
Beware the Creep of Privatisation...
NOT HIS TO SELL
Keep our NHS Public!
National Health Action Party

SAFE IN HIS HANDS, SEVEN DAYS A WEEK
NHS
13-1-16
©Steve Bell 2016-3927.
belltoons.co.uk

"THE NHS WILL
LAST AS LONG
AS THERE ARE
FOLK LEFT WITH
THE FAITH TO
FIGHT FOR IT"
- ANEURIN BEVAN
#TimeToListen

#SAVEOURNHS
HELP US PROTECT
OUR PATIENTS
BMA
BMA
BMA
Junior
doctors'
contract
It's everyone's
fight
Recycling For London Ltd
PROTECT
WE
THE
NHS
#BursaryOrBust
BURSAR

No Bursary
No Opportunity
Socialist Worker
#Bursary OrBust
THESE CUTS WON'T HEAL!
RCN
FALSE
AGAINST
THE
A+E NOT WMD
CLIMATE NOT TRIDENT
NHS NOT TRIDENT
NHS NOT TRIDENT
JOBS NOT
MAFIA

WAR=POVERTY=
NHS
NOT

HOMES
NOT
SAVE THE NHS
SCRAP TRIDENT

A war memorial where the road forks. Men holding a banner:

NO MORE HIROSHIMAS

White letters on black cloth and HONOUR carved in stone. I look at the photograph and imagine that cloth unraveling into a thread stretching back to an August morning more than seventy years ago, a thread that casts a shadow so fine it is invisible, the shadow of mutually assured destruction, the shadow all but forgotten, the shadow under which I have lived my life, seen my children marry, under which I have read stories to my grandchildren as they were drifting off to sleep.

They say we have been safe in the vale of the shadow of weapons too terrible to use.

But the killing ways of war have always kept themselves in shape. Korea, Yemen, Oman, Ukraine, Bosnia, Vietnam, Iraq, the Falklands, Syria, Afghanistan: I cannot list the theatres of conflict where smart bombs and mortars, rocket-propelled grenades and Kalashnikovs, napalm, helicopter gunships, barrel bombs, cruise missiles, IEDs and drones rehearse their lethal respects.

Far, far out at sea, far from the edge of land, even now a submarine is on patrol.

They want us to believe that weapons too terrible to use have kept us safe, have kept us at the top table in the hierarchy of powers.

I remember hearing nearly sixty years ago about tests in Bikini Atoll. In those days the wireless brought the news, the promise of atomic energy was the future and I remember hearing about Japanese fishermen on a boat called Fifth Lucky Dragon. And, as a boy raised on stories of shot-up Lancasters limping home, I modeled a Vulcan bomber innocent of its destructive purpose.

And *"Silly old fool"* I remember someone saying as the TV flickered its grainy black and white images of a white-haired old man addressing Aldermaston marchers in Trafalgar Square. *'Silly old fool'* they said. And I remember the U2 spy plane shot down over Cuba that October when (as they might say now) it nearly all kicked off. And although I do not remember where I heard the story, I think of Sadako Sakasi, born a week before I was, into another coincidence, one of those they call *hibakusha*, folding paper cranes against her dying …

HONOUR
REDHILL & REIGATE
CND
NO MORE
HIROSHIMAS

Do up YOUR TIE
PUT ON A
PROPER SUIT
&
SCRAP
TRIDENT

PEACE
السلام शान्ति: שָׁלוֹם
TO HONOUR
THOSE WHO
SEEK ANOTHER
PATH IN PLACE
OF VIOLENCE
AND WAR
2010
DON'T
BOMB
SYRIA
www.greenparty.org.uk
Green Party
for the common good
Socialist Worker
TORIES WANT NEW MIDDLE EAST WAR
DON'T
BOMB
SYRIA

WE ARE ALL SYRIAN MOTHERS
"...War is the enemy of the Poor"
Martin Luther King
Don't Attack Syria!
Women of Colour Global Strike
A VOTE FOR WAR = MURDER, RAPE + OTHER TORTURE

Stop

SMART BOMBS
DON'T JUSTIFY
DUMB LEADERS

CRIMINAL
BOMBER BLAIR
JAIL THIS WAR
CRIMINAL NOW
OUT,
DAMNED
SPOT

REFUGEES
WHERE
IS ?
YOUR
UMANITY

Socialist Worker

WE WELCOME YOU!
WE WELCOME YOU
TRADE CAMERON for 10,000 REFUGEE
WELCOME REFUSEES
THE WAR

TIME
Refugees

DO NOT OPPRESS THE
STRANGER. YOU WERE
STRANGERS IN EGYPT
REFUG

READY SALTED CRISPS
48 x 32.5ge

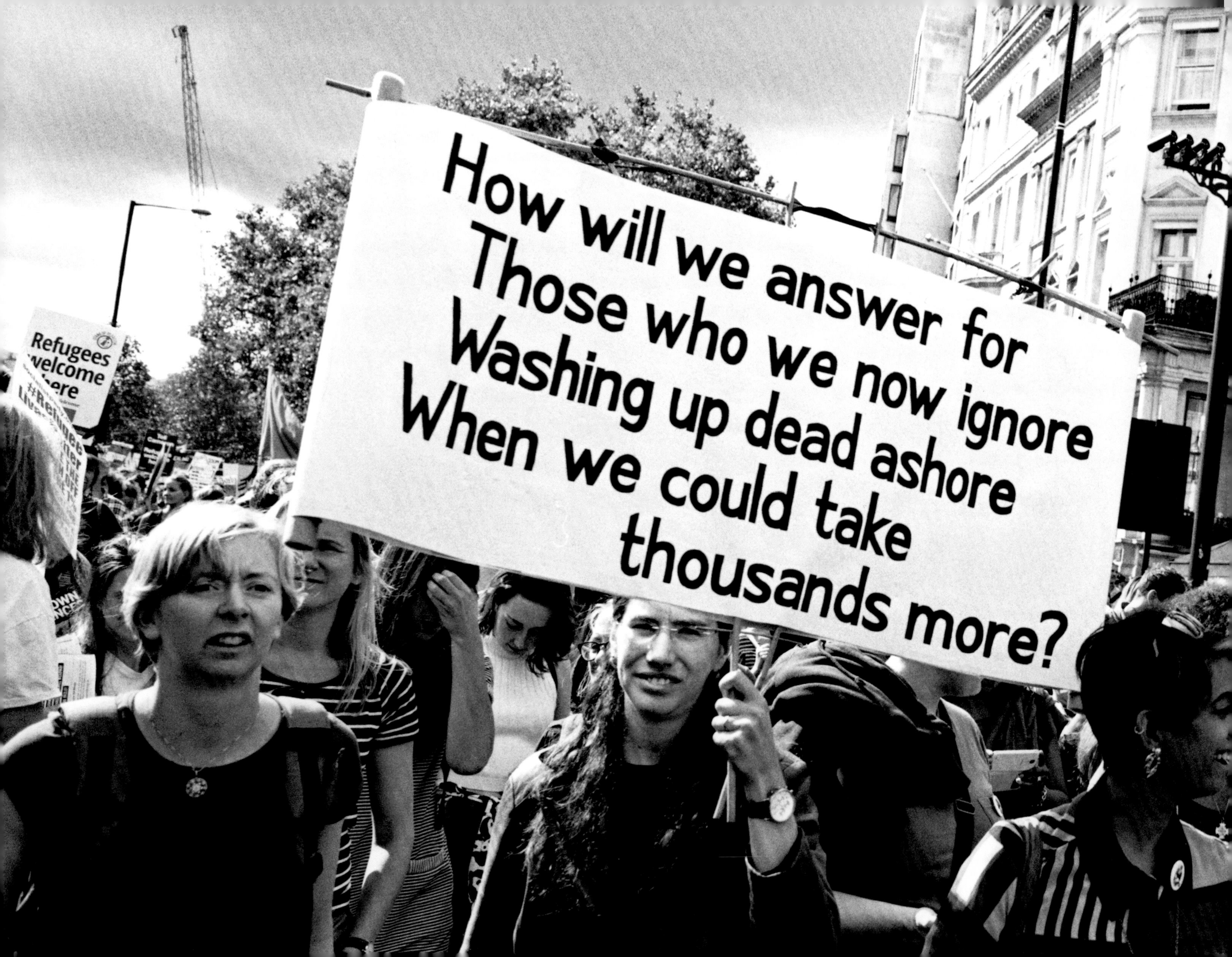
How will we answer for
Those who we now ignore
Washing up dead ashore
When we could take
thousands more?
Refugees
welcome

socialistparty.org.uk
#Refugee LivesMatter
TAKE THE WEALTH OFF THE 1%
FIGHT FOR JOBS, HOMES & SERVICES FOR ALL!
Socialist Party
Tell Cameron
Refugees welcome here
REFUGEES IN
TORIES OUT
THE PEOPLE'S ASSEMBLY
OLD PARK LANE W1
Socialist Worker
REFUGEES WELCOME HERE
Open the borders, let them in
CHOICE
YOU DO

WE ARE ALL REFUGEES
TURKEY NOT SAFE FOR REFUGEES
TURKISH STATE IS RESPONSIBLE FOR ANKARA MASSACRE
KURDISH
CENTRE

ND UP
RACISM
ugees
come
ere
amophobia
-Semitism
pegoating
No to
Islamo
No to
top the War Coalition.
STAND U
TO RAC
Refug
welcon
here
• No to Islamophobia and anti-Semitism
• Stop scapegoating migrants
efugees
elcome
here
No to Islamophobia and anti-Semitism
STAND UP TO RACISM
Refugees welcome here
• No to Islamophobia and anti-Semitism
• Stop scapegoating migrants

NatWes

DO YOU WANT TO
LOOK BACK AND
SAY YOU STOOD BY
AND DID NOTHING?
LET THEM IN!
LONDON
2
CALAIS

I flop into my favoured, comfortable chair, press the red button.

A shipwreck lights up a corner of the living room. Debris awash in Rhodes, desperate figures, sodden humans struggling in the surf. Someone gives a commentary. I happen to know this place at the edge of the sea. Zephyros beach. Not far from the cemetery where I have paid my respects at an open coffin resting in a family grave. How carefully straightened the limbs of loved ones so precisely laid to rest. How carefully tended those ancestral bones...

A man, a woman, a child have drowned, though many are saved. Months later I learn how a woman, pulled pregnant from the sea that day, has given her child their rescuer's name...

Far from the sea, homeward safely by train, half dozing in the quiet zone, the reassurance of familiar stations, Denham, Gerrards Cross, Seer Green and Jordans, Beaconsfield. Onward past High Wycombe and into the Chilterns. A footpath crosses a field. Thoughts drift, the fluid cut and paste of waking dreams, this blessed plot, this earth, this realm, this England, surrounded by the silver sea, which serves it in the office of a wall... policies and placards interwoven in the mind

"Say it loud say it clear refugees are welcome here..."
We need a comprehensive solution...

WHAT IF IT WAS YOU?

... that deals with the people most responsible for the terrible scenes we see: President Assad in Syria, the butchers of ISIL, and the criminal gangs that are running this terrible trade in people.

TRADE CAMERON FOR 10,000 REFUGEES

The partly decomposed bodies of 71 refugees were found piled on top of each other in a truck abandoned on a motorway... the stench of putrefaction...

WOULD YOU HELP ME – IF I WAS A REFUGEE?

...several arrests have been made.

BE A MENSCH   SUPPORT THE REFUGEES

Somewhere in Austria an elderly woman is providing food at her garden gate, she says that when the war ended in 1945 she herself had been a refugee, she says: *"And you never forget."*

WELCOME THE STRANGER IN YOUR MIDST,
FOR SUCH WERE SOME OF YOU

While we must of course provide support to address the immediate situation, we have to make sure we are not doing anything to make the problem worse...

THEY ARE NOT CHASING OUR BENEFITS
THEY ARE FLEEING OUR BOMBS

In the Balkans, column upon column of people struggling northwards in the heat. Tear gas, razor wire, and weldmesh.

CAMINANTE NO HAY CAMINO – SEHACE CAMINO AL ANDAR

If Europe fails on the question of refugees, then it won't be the Europe we wished for.

BROTHER FROM ANOTHER MOTHER

A rain-soaked day, not far from the edge of the sea. In Dover's Market Square, a reassuring landscape: Natwest, Barclays, British Heart Foundation, Dickens Corner, Dover Convenience Store, Lloyds and The Money Shop, Londis and Colonel Sanders.

Two or three chat under an umbrella with WE ARE ALL IMMIGRANTS WE ALL NEED SHELTER printed on its panels.

The fountain plays behind a weldmesh fence where someone has hung a banner:

REFUGEES ARE WELCOME HERE

Near it, captioned, enlarged and laminated, *that* photograph.
The toddler's body face down in the surf at the edge of the sea,

A BOY THAT CHANGED THE WORLD   AYLAN KURDI R.I.P.

Would that the world had changed, that we need not be here.

I follow words on a placard in a photograph, discover their author, Antonio Machado, look up the poem and complete the stanza:

Caminante, no hay camino, sino estelas en la mar.

Wanderer, there is no road, only foam trails on the sea.

VOTE REMAIN
VOTE REMAIN
VOTE REMAIN
VOTE REMAIN

Leave
Vote Leave

The Lying
COCKWOMBLES
FUCK THIS, I'M MOVING TO
NO BREXIT

BREXSHIT
EU'RE My HERO
WE ARE ALL IMMIGRANTS

YOUR COUNTRY NEEDS
EU

We are far more united and have far more in common than that which divides us.

Jo Cox

FORTUNE AND DISCONTENT

Perhaps it is not the wind that rattles the bedroom window disturbing my dreamless sleep, perhaps it is the clamour of a distant crowd that rattles the panes. Perhaps even now there is a crowd flowing out of Cavendish Square, crying out for dolphins; a crowd flowing out of Portland Place, chanting *"Free free Palestine"*; a crowd flowing past the Dorchester Hotel chanting *"Refugees are welcome here"*; a crowd flowing by the river, past Campaigning Choirs singing in defence of public services, past a banner begging

SUPPORT THE RESISTANCE OF KOBANE AGAINST ISIS ATTACKS

past the music system pumping out *"Which side are you on boys, which side are you on?"*
and someone carrying a sign

IF YOU PRETEND TO PAY US
WE'LL PRETEND TO WORK

Perhaps it is the crowd I saw flowing down the Strand past the Savoy

DEAR TORIES IT'S NOT YOU IT'S ME – JUST KIDDING IT'S YOU

Perhaps it is the voice of a crowd, though I had not thought that anger and conviction could have found so many

AUSTERITY IS NOT A NECESSITY IT IS A POLITICAL CHOICE

'But there are conventions which are generally accepted by the demonstrators on one side and the authorities on the other

20 MILLION VOTERS DIDN'T VOTE TORY

'The protestors behave with a sense of proportion and do not cause excessive damage or inconvenience

A SPOT OF ANARCHY WOULD BE NICE?

'and they vouch the sincerity of their beliefs by accepting the penalties imposed by the law

SHAME THE MEDIA WON'T LET YOU SEE THIS

'The police and prosecutors, on the other hand, behave with restraint and the magistrates impose sentences which take the conscientious motives of the protestors into account.'

IF THIS PROTEST WAS IN EGYPT YOU'D END UP
KILLED INJURED DETAINED

And a crowd in Cardiff was marching down Castle Street to Jubilee Park with placards in my grandmother's language

TEGWCH I BALESINA! CICIWCH ISRAEL ALLAN O UEFA

because Wales were playing Israel and

THE KOP SAY KICK ISRAEL OUT OF UEFA AND FIFA

and in front of me a banner backlit in mirror writing

SNAINITSELAP ROF ECITSUJ ROF SWEJ

which, keeping pace with the crowd, I decipher

JEWS FOR JUSTICE FOR PALESTINIANS

There was a woman there, I remember, wearing a keffiyeh. She had made a doll-child and bloodied it with paint and along the route between neat undamaged terraces she clutched it to her breast, while another time in a crowd in Luton a young couple stood with their defiance

NO TO FASCIST BRITAIN FIRST

while all around were chanting *"Britain First are Britain's worst"* and the mother kissed her baby daughter and told me "We're here because of her."

And a crowd in Leicester protesting against the badger cull found itself delayed in Town Hall Square by a wedding party; the newlyweds asked to be photographed among a backdrop of campaigners and I wonder who caught the bouquet the bride tossed over her shoulder.

*****

And the crowd's roar in the city where walls reflected in the dark gloss of windows reminded me of a retired bricklayer I once met; he told me how he liked to show his children and grandchildren the brickwork he'd laid in his home town. And I think of his pride in his work and of the joshing among the steel workers I met in Whitehall Gardens and wonder how torturers account for their days, or what daddy says when he has spent his day in one of those secret regions where, as Auden wrote, *'good family men keep eye, devoted as monks, on apparatus in which harmless matter turns homicidal.'*

And on one of those days of autumn sunlight that has the bees in flight around my eaves I met a man who'd made a placard of his fortune and his discontent

ME:
BORN IN THE 40'S
EDUCATION – FREE
HOME – BOUGHT A HOUSE AT 23
GRANDKIDS:
BORN IN THE NOUGHTIES,
EDUCATION – £40,000 DEBT
HOME – THE BEST THEY'LL GET IS A BUY TO LET
WHO'S ETON ALL THE PIES DAVE?

Shall we define hypocrisy as *'preaching permanent austerity from behind a golden lectern'* or austerity as *'punishing the poor for the mistakes of the rich'*?

ARE YOU HAPPY WITH THINGS THE WAY THEY ARE?

RECLAIM OUR DEMOCRACY FROM THE 5 MEDIA BILLIONAIRES

RICH PARENTS FOR ALL

and

ALL I WANNA SAY IS THAT THEY DON'T REALLY CARE ABOUT US

and always bear in mind

YOUR SILENCE GIVES CONSENT

❄❄❄❄❄

In Old Palace Yard on Magna Carta Day I stumbled on two placards propped up against each other

MAGNA CARTA PUTS GOVERNMENT UNDER AUTHORITY OF GOD

FREEDOM EQUALITY & DIVERSITY FOR ALL

and out near Bedford I read a banner that reframed a trophy-hunter's kill

CECIL SAYS ALL HUMANS ARE BORN FREE

and on Northumberland Avenue I saw a gathering of people demanding

NIGERIA FIGHT CORRUPTION NOT GAYS

STOP ARRESTS OF LGBTI PEOPLE

And the door of the Embassy slammed shut against their petition.

Then one day near All Souls Church in Langham Place I met a young man who'd made a sign

BOMBING FOR PEACE IS LIKE FUCKING FOR VIRGINITY

and in Park Lane another time a woman owning a story that spoke to history

MY 4 GREAT GRANDADS FOUGHT IN WWI
MY 2 GRANDADS FOUGHT IN WWII
3 OF MY GREAT UNCLES WENT TO CONCENTRATION CAMPS
THIS IS WHY I VOTED REMAIN

So perhaps it is the jubilation of the Brexiteers that is disturbing my sleep, or the engine of the campaign bus rattling the coffers of the NHS as I wake up to wonder what their mantra **TAKE BACK CONTROL** might turn out to mean. For they, as Yeats once said, *'had fed the heart on fantasies'*, and we may yet discover exactly how *'the heart's grown brutal from the fare'*. So I thank the friend who told me he'd seen a **VOTE LEAVE** sign altered to read **VOTE LOVE**; he took me and my camera back to the place but it had already been removed. But a fortnight later, travelling up the motorway at seventy miles an hour, I saw a row of **REMAIN** placards on a rising bank. And long after I had passed I imagined their shapes as a convoy of trucks on a distant hillside, and an unbidden image flashed up: destruction in a barren land. And I remember driving to Lincolnshire where Royal Air Force officers, intent as surgeons, are piloting drones, are keeping eye on mountainous roads or compounds and deciphering people by the heat of their flesh. Their targets are far away but here outside the fence there was a banner strung up between a couple of trees

DRONES DESTROY OUR HUMANITY

Someone was selling blue scarves made in Afghanistan, blue the colour of the sky that arches over us all. There was a picnic with food to share because we would have scones not drones and a skype call to a peace group in Kabul who, among the horrors, are not forgotten. Between worlds linked for compassion or destruction by the wonders of satellite technology, their features buffered and jerked upon our screen.

EVERY AFGHAN HAS A NAME – WAR IS NOT A VIDEO GAME

✻✻✻✻✻

But there are holidays abroad, cash in the attic, a place in the country, and football, and celebrity weddings or an outing to Disneyworld, and a flat screen TV where the immaculately dressed newsreaders warn that reports *'contain images which some viewers may find distressing'*; betraying no emotion as back-projected gunfire plays out in ruined streets and refugees stumble from dinghies behind them. And once more in parliament there is another assurance about the big society and how the economy is growing but over the crowds I have seen placards floating like speech bubbles

HEALTH CARE WEALTH SHARE

and someone carrying a sign

IF YOU CAN FIND MONEY TO KILL PEOPLE
YOU CAN FIND MONEY TO HEAL PEOPLE

And if you don't want to know the final scores, look away now. Or search out the place to which the bearers of bad tidings escape and, losing their composure, fall upon the earth and cover their heads with ashes and rend their garments in mourning because

LOOKING AWAY WON'T MAKE IT GO AWAY

✻✻✻✻✻

Perhaps it is not after all the wind rattling the panes that lifts me into dreams; perhaps it is the belly laughter of a cruel god watching a continuous loop of calamity in which the little children with hollowed eyes and big bellies and bow legs are too weak to stand or to hold up a bowl crudely inscribed *EVERY LIFE IS PRECIOUS*. A cruel god watching as the traffickers ignore the cries of the gulls, and the deep sea-swell rolls over the profits of cash in hand and the loss of the boats is none of their business as currents under the sea pick the bones of the drowned in whispers....

WE ARE ALL IN THE SAME BOAT: EVERY LIFE IS PRECIOUS

*****

Then when MPs were about to vote on extending bombing missions into Syria I saw protestors standing in the rain by a tablet of stone with the word PEACE repeated in Arabic, Hebrew, and Sanskrit. And once on a march I saw swinging from a pole a bloodied totem and a text that read: *'This bag of meat represents the mangled bodies of children and adults ripped apart by Israeli explosives. Appalled? You should be! Disgusted? You should be! Insensitive? War does not respect sensitivities!'* And I remember the dignity of a woman holding a placard

A VOTE FOR WAR = MURDER, RAPE AND OTHER TORTURE

and all I can do is hope that someone will upload videos of protests like these onto social media so the victims of oppression and injustice will know they are not without some demonstration of support ...

And I read old words on a new placard: *'That which is hateful to you, do not do to your neighbour. That is the whole Torah, the rest is commentary.'*

Perhaps what disturbs me is the memory of a helicopter circling above Trafalgar Square. That day, from a temporary rostrum, someone was telling a crowd about the deliberate targeting of hospitals, doctors, and medical supplies in Syria because removing any hope of help or care is a way to weaken the will of the people. And there was a woman there who had come on crutches from Downing Street with her sign

OH WORLD ... HAVE YOU HAD YOUR FILL OF SYRIAN CHILDREN'S BLOOD?!

That was the day the police cordoned off a corner of the square; and when the helicopter landed it was the air ambulance, coming, they told me, to an accident. Then when the noise died down the speaker resumed, talking of injuries, talking of barrel bombs, the destruction of hospitals, the killing of doctors ...

But tonight it is the drub-drub-drubbing beat of rotors that rattles the windows, that evokes these images; a Chinook flying fast and low across the Oxfordshire landscape, over hay-barns and beech woods, over fattening cattle and this year's lambs, while somewhere far out at sea, far from the edge of land, a submarine is on patrol, running silent, running deep. Exactly who knows where? Perhaps dolphins and whales and other creatures of the sea are aware of its presence. In its safe, we are told, are the sealed orders to be read when deterrence has failed. What might they say? *'There's not much to come home to, it's all down to you, lads. Take revenge if you must, though we can't say where or what good it will do. So why not just break out the Scotch, sing Rule Britannia one last time, and scuttle the ship?'*

And I remember talking to a man selling *The Big Issue* in St Martins Lane. Yes, he said without any rancour, yes, he'd seen the people go past with their signs saying **REFUGEES WELCOME**, but none had stopped to speak to him, or to buy a copy of the magazine.

And I think of the woman I saw standing alone watching the steel workers march past parliament, all in their working gear. And she was there, oblivious to those beside and behind her who must have had their own urgencies to go to; she was there, she was simply there, clapping the men as they passed.

❋❋❋❋❋

But then again perhaps after all it was only the wind, only the wind that shook my window, that unsettled my sleep so that with absolute clarity I remembered the two young students, two girls from Stoke Newington and the message they carried, *'There may be times when we are powerless to prevent injustice, but there must never be a time when we fail to protest.'*

John Comino-James
November 2016

INDEX TO THE PHOTOGRAPHS

55
After the attack at the Riu Imperial Marhaba Hotel near Sousse, Tunisia
Trafalgar Square, London, 4 July 2015

58
Demonstrations on the occasion of the vote on the Assisted Dying Bill
Old Palace Yard, Westminster, London, 11 September 2015

60-61
During the UK visit of the Chinese President Xi-Jinping
The Mall, London, 20 October 2015

63
Taiji Action Day March
Piccadilly Circus, London, 19 February 2016

65
Global March for Lions
Cavendish Square, London, 30 April 2016

66
Compassion in World Farming #AnimalsAreNotFreight
Parliament Square, London, 29 August 2016

67
Keep the Ban on fox hunting
Whitehall, London, 15 July 2015

69
38 Degrees: Save our Bees protest
Whitehall, London, 7 July 2015

70-71
38 Degrees: Stop TTIP protest
Norwich, 22 August 2015

72-73
#OccupyDemocracy
Parliament Square, London, 20 December 2014

75, 76-77
People's Assembly Anti-Austerity March
Parliament Square, London, 20 June 2015

78-79
Free Education Student demonstration
Whitehall. London, 4 November 2015

80-81
The People's Assembly: Protest the Tory Party Conference
Manchester, 4 October 2015

82
The People's Assembly: Protest the Tory Party Conference
Manchester, 4 October 2015
Disabled People Against Cuts: Balls to the Budget
Whitehall, London, 8 July 2015

83
People's Assembly Anti-Austerity March
Parliament Square, London, 20 June 2015
Disabled People Against Cuts: Balls to the Budget
Whitehall, London, 8 July 2015

86
People's Assembly Anti-Austerity March
Fleet Street, London, 20 June 2015
No Privatisation at the National Gallery
Trafalgar Square, London, 30 May2015

87
People's Assembly Anti-Austerity March
Parliament Square, London, 20 June 2015
Kill the Housing Bill
Lincolns Inn Fields, London, 13 March 2016

88-89
Kill the Bill - Protect the Right to Strike
Westminster Hall, London, 2 November 2015

90
Liberal Democrats protest against Conservative plans to scrap the Human Rights Act
Whitehall, London, 30 May 2015

91
The People's Assembly: Protest the Tory Party Conference
Manchester, October 2015
People's Assembly Anti-Austerity March
City of London, 20 June 2015

92-93
The People's Assembly: Protest the Tory Party Conference
Manchester, October 2015

94
Free Education Student demonstration
London, 4 November 2015
The People's Assembly: Protest the Tory Party Conference
Manchester, October 2015

95
People's Assembly Anti-Austerity March
City of London 20 June 2015
Free Education Student demonstration
London, 4 November 2015

96-97
Demonstration against the Housing and Planning Bill
Lincolns Inn Fields, London, 13 March 2016

98-99
Save our Steel protest
Whitehall Gardens, London, 25 May 2016

100-101
People's Assembly Anti-Austerity March
Parliament Square, London, 20 June 2015

102
Protest against fracking in the Forest of Dean
Shire Hall, Gloucester, September 2015

103
People's Climate March
Whitehall, London, 21 September 2014

104-105
Campaign against Climate Change
Park Lane, London, 29 November 2015

106-107
Plane Stupid protest at the Conservative Party Conference
Manchester, 5 October 2015

109
Supporters of the Heathrow 13
Willesden Magistrates Court, 24 February 2016

110-111
Disabled People Against Cuts: Balls to the Budget
Whitehall, London, 8 July 2015

112-113
People's March for the NHS
The Strand, London, 6 September 2014

114-115
Junior Doctors' protest
Waterloo Place, London, 6 February 2016

116
Junior Doctors' picket
Headley Way, Oxford, 12 January 2016
Nurses' Bursary protest
York Road, London, 9 January 2016

117
Nurses' Bursary protest,
Waterloo Bridge, London, 9 January 2016
Campaign for Nuclear Disarmament: Wrap up Trident
Horse Guards Avenue, London, 26 January 2015

118-119
Campaign for Nuclear Disarmament: Wrap up Trident
Victoria Embankment, London, 26 January 2015

121
Hiroshima Day - 70th Anniversary
Reigate and Redhill Campaign for Nuclear Disarmament
Near Redhill, Surrey, 6 August 2015

123
Campaign for Nuclear Disarmament: Scrap Trident March
Trafalgar Square, 27 February 2016

125
Stop the War Coalition: Don't Bomb Syria
Bonn Square, Oxford, 28 November 2015

126-127
Stop the War Coalition: Don't Bomb Syria
Portland Place, London, 12 December 2015

128-129
Campaign for Nuclear Disarmament: Scrap Trident march
Marble Arch, London, 27 February 2016

130-131
Publication of the Chilcot Report
Broad Sanctuary, Westminster, London, 6 July 2016

132-133
Refugees Welcome
Park Lane, London, 12 September 2015

134-135
Refugees Welcome
Piccadilly, London, 12 September 2015

136-137
Refugees Welcome
Park Lane, London, 12 September 2015

138-139
Refugees Welcome
Piccadilly, London, 12 September 2015

140-141
Stand up to Racism and Fascism
Portland Place, London 21 March 2016

142-143
Refugees Welcome
Market Square, Dover, 17 October 2015

147
Vote Remain
M40, Oxfordshire, 30 July 2016
Vote Leave
B4009, Aston Rowant, Oxfordshire, 17 July 2016

149
March for Europe
Park Lane, London, 2 July 2016
March for Europe
Near Parliament Square, London, 2 July 2016

151
March for Europe
Near Parliament Square, London, 2 July 2016

NOTES ON THE TEXTS

I have photographed extensively at demonstrations over a two-year period beginning in July 2014. Many of the events at which I have photographed are not directly represented in this book, and the majority of the images I collected do not exist as finished prints but only in an archive of negatives and contact sheets. It is this archive, as well as passing conversations and observations, that I have used extensively as source material when writing the texts.

ACKNOWLEDGEMENTS

My thanks to Peter Rhoades, Lucy Walters, John Blakemore, Brian Woolland, and Dewi Lewis for their encouragement and suggestions as this work took shape.

And I am, as ever, grateful to Anna for her continuing faith in my work, for challenging my use of syntax, and for relieving me of so many of the vicissitudes of daily life.

BIOGRAPHY

Born in Somerset, John Comino-James lives near Thame in Oxfordshire. He has published seven previous books of photographs:

Nearly Every Tuesday, which documented Thame's weekly street market; *Fairground Attraction*, which explored the way of life of travelling showmen; *A Few Streets, a Few People*, an intimate portrait of the people and surroundings of the Cayo Hueso barrio in Havana, Cuba; *In a Very English Town*, which acknowledges qualities that typify Thame as an English market town; *Fortunate Steps*, photographs made in Havana's historic Calzada del Diez de Octubre; *Havana, Intimations of Departure*; and most recently, *A Question of England*.

His work has been exhibited in Thame, Oxford, London and Havana.

SHOUT IT LOUD, SHOUT IT CLEAR
John Comino-James

First published in the
United Kingdom in 2017 by

Dewi Lewis Publishing
8 Broomfield Road
Heaton Moor
Stockport SK4 4ND
England

www.dewilewis.com

ISBN: 978-1-911306-09-2

Design and Layout: Dewi Lewis and John Comino-James
Print: EBS, Verona, Italy